Henry VIII

...and his six wives

Sarah Ridley

W

FRANKLIN WATTS
LONDON•SYDNEY

First published in 2009 by
Franklin Watts
338 Euston Road
London NW1 3BH

Franklin Watts Australia
Level 17/207 Kent Street
Sydney NSW 2000

Series editor: Jeremy Smith
Art director: Jonathan Hair
Design: Simon Morse
Cover Design: Jonathan Hair
Picture research: Sarah Ridley

Picture credits: Berger Collection, Denver
Art Museum/Getty Images: 11.
Bridgeman Art Library /Getty Images: 22,
23. EH/HIP/Topfoto: 20.
Robert Harding/Getty Images: 15.
Hever Castle, Kent/Bridgeman Art Library:
16. Hulton Archive/Getty Images: 4, 9.
Imagno/Austrian Archives/Hulton
Archive/Getty Images: 8, 18. Kingston
Lacy/Bridgeman Art Library: 5. Magdalene
College, Cambridge/Eileen Tweedy/Picture
Desk:13. Musée du Chateau de Versailles
/Gianni Dagli Orti/Picture Desk: 12. Musée
du Louvre Paris/Gianni Dagli Orti/Picture
Desk: 21. NPG London/Bridgeman Art
Library: 14. Picturepoint/Topham: 19.
Private Collection/Bridgeman Art Library:
6, 7. R Sheridan/AA&A Collection: 10.
Taxi/Getty Images: 17.
Topfoto: 1. Walker Art Gallery & National
Museums, Liverpool/Bridgeman Art
Library: front cover.

Dewey classification: 942.05'2'092
ISBN 978 0 7496 8709 0

A CIP catalogue record for this book is
available from the British Library

Printed in China

Franklin Watts is a division of
Hachette Children's Books,
an Hachette UK company.
www.hachette.co.uk

Contents

The Tudor family

In 1491 Henry Tudor was born into the royal Tudor family. He was the second son of King Henry VII and his wife, Elizabeth of York.

A portrait of Henry Tudor. He would become King Henry VIII.

1485

Henry Tudor becomes Henry VII, King of England.

1486

Arthur Tudor is born.

Henry grew up with his brother, Arthur, and sisters, Margaret and Mary. They lived in royal palaces in London or close by.

Henry was born in Greenwich Palace, close to the city of London.

Childhood

Henry was a clever boy. He learnt to read and write in English, Latin and ancient Greek. A teacher came to the palace to teach the royal children.

Tudor children used hornbooks to learn to read.

1501 ▶

Arthur marries Catherine of Aragon, a Spanish princess.

1502 ▶

Arthur dies.

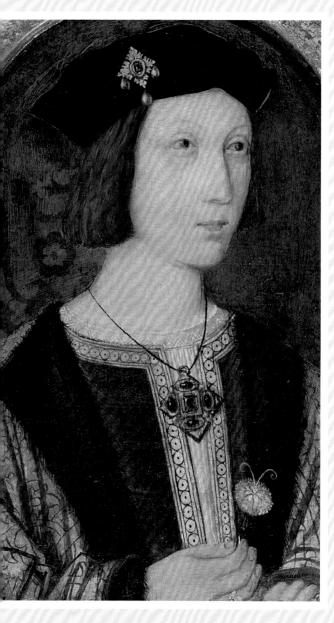

Henry's brother, Arthur, learnt how to be a king as well. Sadly, when he was only 16, Arthur fell ill and died. Now Henry would be the next ruler of England.

A portrait of Arthur Tudor, Henry's brother.

1503 ▶

It is agreed that Henry will marry Catherine of Aragon.

The coronation

In 1509, Henry VII died. His advisors suggested that the new king, Henry VIII, marry Catherine of Aragan, the daughter of the king and queen of Spain.

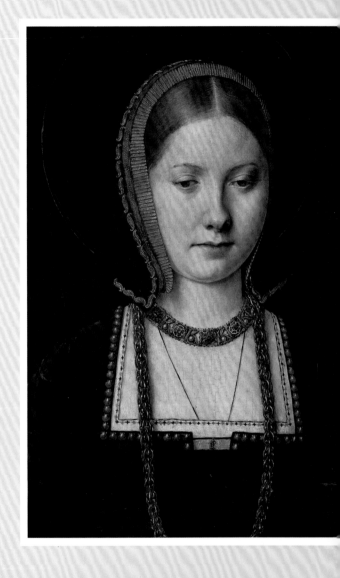

A portrait of Catherine of Aragon, Arthur's widow and a Spanish princess.

April
1509

Henry VII dies.

April
1509

Henry becomes king, aged 17.

This drawing shows the coronation of King Henry and Queen Catherine.

Although he was not keen at first, Henry knew it was necessary to improve relations with Spain. The marriage took place and the coronation soon afterwards.

11th June
1509 ▶

Henry marries Catherine of Aragon. She is five years older than him.

24th June
1509 ▶

The coronation takes place.

The young king

Henry was a handsome, active young man. He enjoyed hunting on horseback, jousting and playing tennis. He also liked to play music, read and write.

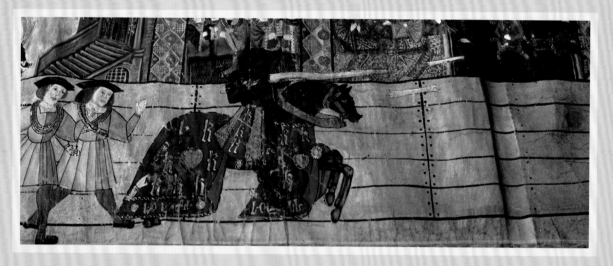

Jousts were contests between knights.

January
1510 ▶

Henry takes part in his first joust.

There were
many dances
and feasts at
the royal court.
The court was
the group of
people who
gathered
around the
king.

▶ This painting shows Henry as
a slim young man.

Catherine of Aragon has a son,
Henry, but he lives for just 52 days.

War and peace

Henry wanted England to be a strong country in Europe. To do that, he added ships to the navy and went to war with France and Scotland.

The *Mary Rose* was one of Henry's favourite warships.

1513 ▷

The English are at war with Scotland and France.

1514 ▷

Thomas Wolsey becomes chief minister.

1516 ▷

Princess Mary is born.

This painting shows Henry on horseback, arriving at the Field of the Cloth of Gold in France, to make peace with the French king.

Back at home, Henry let his ministers run the country most of the time. In 1520 his chief minister, Thomas Wolsey, arranged a meeting with the King of France to make peace.

1519 ►

Ferdinand Magellan and his crew sail around the world.

1520 ►

The Field of the Cloth of Gold meeting in France.

13

A son for Henry

Thomas Wolsey ran the country well but he was not popular.

Henry longed for a son to rule after him. When Henry fell in love with a woman called Anne Boleyn, he asked Thomas Wolsey to get him a divorce from Catherine.

1521 ▷

Henry writes a book about religion.

1526 ▷

Henry has been married to Catherine of Aragon for 17 years.

Thomas Wolsey pleaded with the Pope, the head of the Roman Catholic Church, to grant Henry a divorce. The Pope refused and Henry was so angry that he took away Wolsey's power.

Thomas Wolsey built Hampton Court Palace and Henry took it over.

1526 ▶

Henry falls in love with a young woman called Anne Boleyn.

1529 ▶

Thomas Wolsey loses power.

Henry and the Church

Henry was a religious man. However, he decided to break contact with the Roman Catholic Church and make himself head of the new Church of England.

Henry was in love with Anne Boleyn for several years.

1533 ▶	September 1533 ▶
Henry divorces Catherine and marries Anne Boleyn.	Princess Elizabeth is born.

Now he could grant himself a divorce from Catherine of Aragon and marry Anne. She gave birth to a baby girl, Elizabeth. Sadly, he soon tired of Anne and he gave the order for her to be executed in 1536.

1534 ▶

Henry becomes head of the Church of England.

1536 ▶

Henry divorces Anne Boleyn and has her executed.

A third wife

Jane Seymour gave Henry the son he longed for.

Henry married his third wife, Jane Seymour, in 1536. The next year she had a son, Edward, but she died soon afterwards. Henry was heart-broken.

1535 ▷

Start of the Laws in Wales Acts, which unify Wales and England.

1536 ▷

Henry marries Jane Seymour.

Now that Henry was head of the Church of England, he wanted to destroy the link with the Pope. One way of doing this was to close down all the monasteries.

The ruins of some monasteries still survive, including Fountains Abbey in Yorkshire.

1536-1540

Henry closes down monasteries and nunneries.

1537

Jane Seymour gives birth to Prince Edward and dies soon afterwards.

A return to war

In the 1540s, Henry went to war with France again. As he needed to make alliances, his ministers thought it would be good if Henry married a German next, Anne of Cleves.

Henry built several forts and castles to defend England from France.

1540s
Henry gives orders for several castles to be built.

January
1540
Henry marries and Anne of Cleves.

Henry found Anne of Cleves dull and divorced her. He married his fifth wife, Catherine Howard, in the same year. When Henry found out she had a lover, he gave orders for her to be executed.

Henry felt tricked into marrying Anne of Cleves by this painting. She was not as pretty in real life.

July
1540
Henry divorces Anne of Cleves and marries Catherine Howard.

1541
Henry makes himself King of Ireland.

1542
Catherine Howard is executed.

Old age

Old, fat and ill, Henry married for the final time in 1543. His new wife, Catherine Parr, cared for him until he died at the age of 56.

This painting of Henry shows him looking huge and powerful.

1543 ▷
Henry marries
Catherine Parr.

1545 ▷
The *Mary Rose*
warship sinks.

28 January
1547 ▷
Henry dies.

This painting shows Henry VIII, Jane Seymour and Edward in the centre. His daughter Mary and Philip II of Spain are pictured on the left.

His only son became King Edward VI. After Edward died, Henry's daughters ruled as Queen Mary I and Queen Elizabeth I. The Tudor times came to an end in 1603 when Elizabeth died.

1547

Edward Tudor is crowned Edward VI.

1553

Mary Tudor is crowned Mary I.

1558

Elizabeth Tudor is crowned Elizabeth I.

Glossary

Church of England The Church created by Henry VIII in 1534. The king or queen of England is the head of this Church, rather than the Pope.

Divorce This legally ends a marriage.

Execution Putting a prisoner to death.

Hornbook Words or letters marked on wood and protected by a thin layer of animal horn, used to learn to read.

Ministers Powerful people who help run the country.

Monasteries Places where monks and nunds lived and worshipped God.

Navy The armed ships of a country.

Pope The head of the Roman Catholic Church who lives in Rome, Italy.

Tennis Tudors played a version of indoor tennis called 'real tennis'.

Index